Wrapping Day at the North Pole

by Ginger R. Burrows

One week before Santa loads up his sleigh with toys, the elves have their own special holiday called Wrapping Day.

Wrapping Day is when all the elves get to choose the Christmas paper they will use to wrap the toys they have made

over the whole year;
and then wrap them all
up! Each elf only gets
to choose one paper,
so that paper must be
special to

them. This day is a fun filled festival that includes a feast, elf games, and toy wrapping.

All the Christmas paper in the world comes from the magical Christmas Paper Forest in the North Pole. This forest is very special, so special that there are only two keys to the huge gate that guards the forest; Santa has one key, and the other one

belongs to Jolly Elf.

Jolly is in charge of

the whole forest, and

all the Christmas

papers in the

world, so he has a very important job! Christmas Paper Forest is not like any other forest in the world; it is magical! There are thousands of Christmas paper trees in this forest, and each tree grows different paper. The design on the paper comes from whatever type of tree is growing it. If the paper it grows has candy ribbon on it, then the tree is

made of candy ribbon. There are Snowmen trees, Snowflake trees, Gum Drop trees, Reindeer trees, Candy Cane trees,

Gift box trees, and thousands more. The tree branches grow sheets of Christmas paper that twirl down and the paper is

harvested by the
Lumber Elves.
The Lumber Elves are a
group of elves that
live in Christmas Paper
Forest.

There are thousands of Lumber Elves, and they take care of all the Christmas Paper trees. A week before Wrapping

Day, Jolly Elf walks through the forest and chooses what Christmas paper will be harvested for the season.

On Wrapping Day, before the elf feast and elf games, Jolly lays out all the beautiful Christmas Paper for each elf to choose. There are no two types of papers alike, and each elf can only choose one for all their toys. When all the

elves have chosen
their special paper,
the wrapping festival
begins.
During the wrapping
festival, the elves
wrap

gifts, sing, dance, and have Mrs. Claus's homemade cookies, brownies, and milk. The elves look forward to this fun filled day all year long, and then, they load up all the presents into Santa's bag for his big Christmas Eve trip around the world.

SANTA'S WORKSHOP
ELF VILLAGE
Reindeer Crossing
Candy Cane LANE

So, children, go look
under your Christmas
tree, and see if the
same Christmas paper
is on more than one
gift, if it

is, you know that the same elf wrapped it!

The End